2019 U.S.A. Calendar – Alaska Outdoor Photos

(Full Moon Dates = ☺)

Copyright © 2018 Daniel H. Wieczorek & Kazuya Numazawa

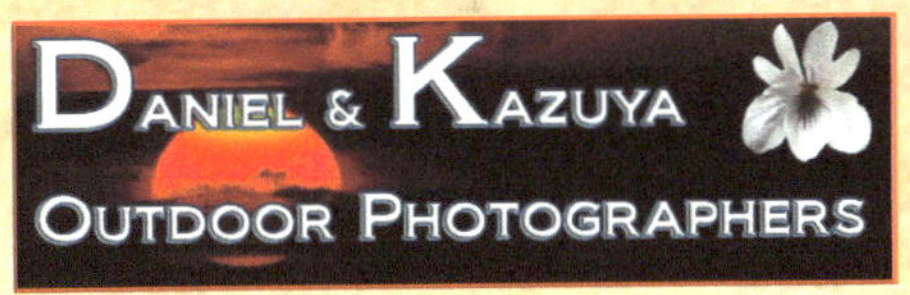

ALL RIGHTS RESERVED. This calendar contains material protected under International and Federal Copyright Laws and Treaties. Any unauthorized reprint or use of this material is prohibited. No part of this calendar may be reproduced or transmitted in any form or by any means, electronic or mechanical, including photocopying, recording, or by any information storage and retrieval system without express written permission from the authors.

ISBN-10: 0-9969810-8-X
ISBN-13: 978-0-9969810-8-8

PHOTOS INCLUDED IN THIS CALENDAR

January: A beautiful early afternoon snow scene near Fairbanks, Alaska.
February: A 12:23 PM snow scene at the University of Alaska - Fairbanks, Alaska, West Ridge.
March: A 6:59 PM sunset scene on the Vernal Equinox near Fairbanks, Alaska.
April: Caribou (*Rangifer tarandus*) on the move near Eagle Summit, Alaska.
May: An incredible mountain scene in the Alaska Range, from near Summit Lake, Alaska.
June: Calypso Orchids (*Calypso bulbosa* var. *americana*) near Fairbanks, Alaska.
July: Spotted Lady's Slipper Orchids (*Cypripedium guttatum*) at Grapefruit Rocks near Fairbanks, Alaska.
August: *Castilleja elegans* (Elegant Indian Paintbrush) at Wickersham Dome near Fairbanks, Alaska.
September: Grizzly (Brown) Bear (*Ursus arctos horribilis*) near Eagle Summit, Alaska.
October: The Northern Lights (Aurora Borealis) near Fairbanks, Alaska.
November: A cozy log house near Fairbanks, Alaska.
December: Birch tree shadows on the snow near Fairbanks, Alaska.

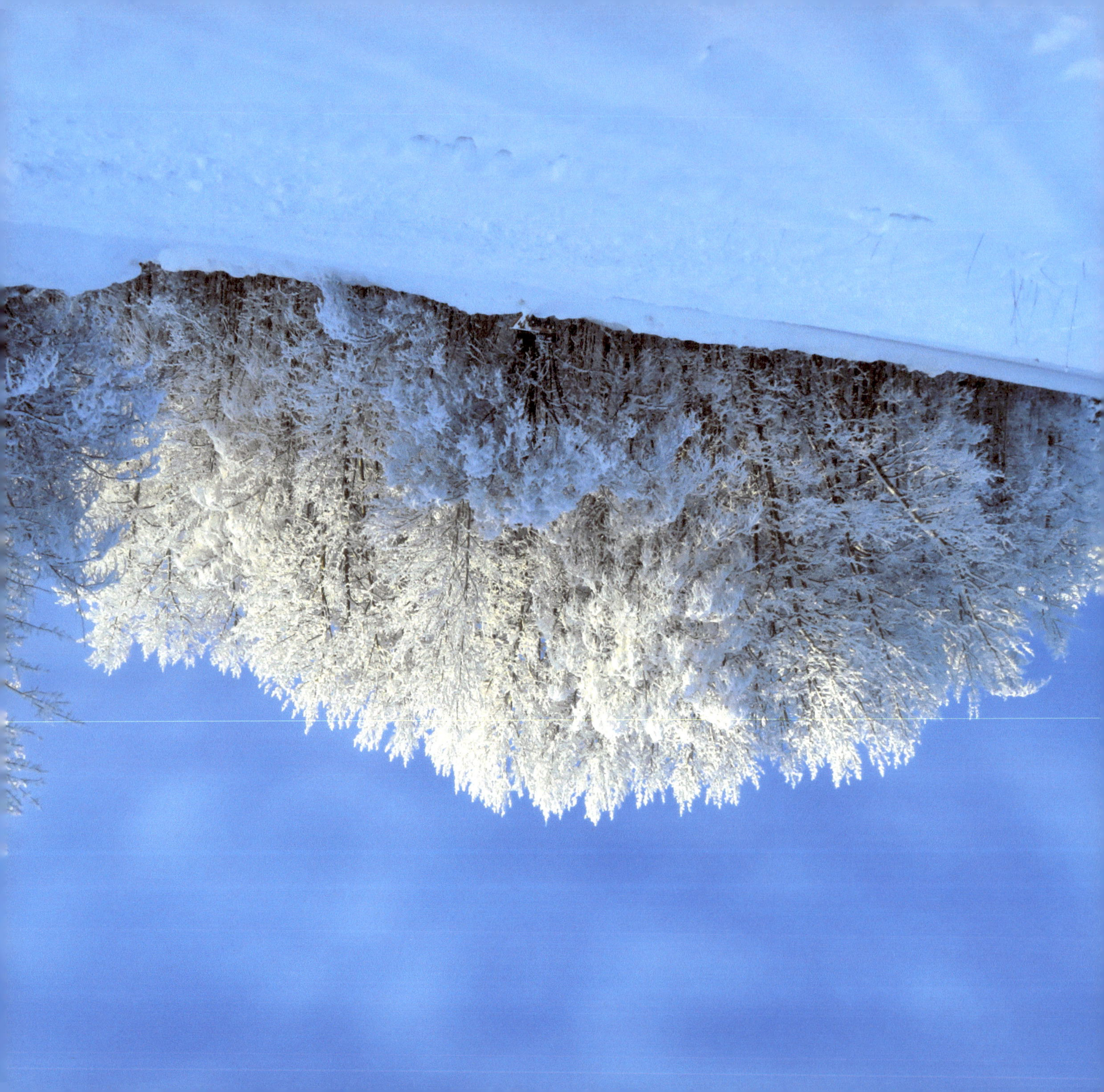

January 2019

Sun	Mon	Tue	Wed	Thu	Fri	Sat
30	31	1 New Year's Day	2	3	4	5
6	7	8	9	10	11	12
13	14	15	16	17	18	19
20	Martin Luther King Day	22	23	24	25	26
27	28	29	30	31	1	2

A beautiful early afternoon snow scene near Fairbanks, Alaska.

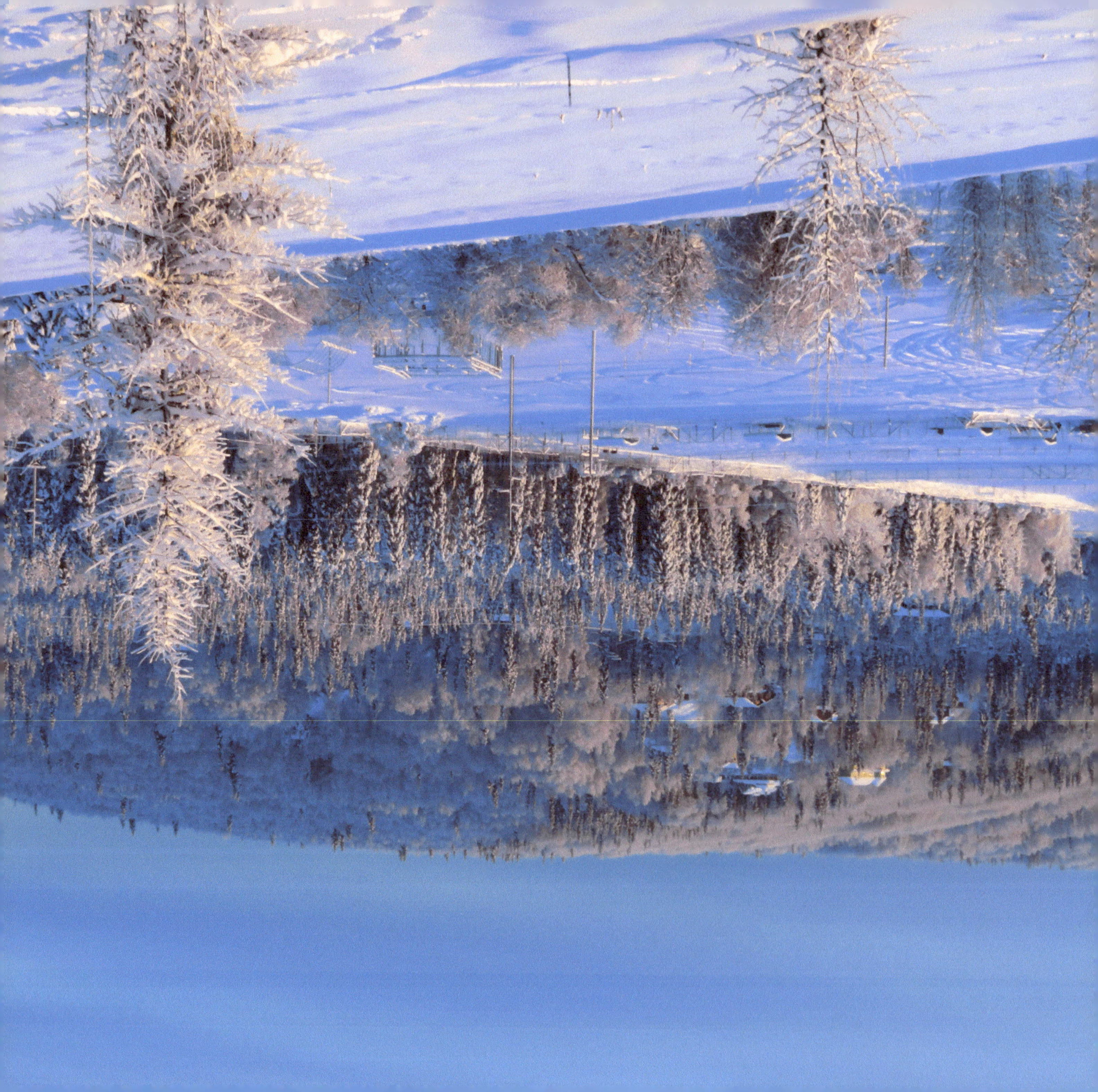

February 2019

Sun	Mon	Tue	Wed	Thu	Fri	Sat
27	28	29	30	31	1	2
3	4	5	6	7	8	9
10	11	12	13	14 Valentine's Day	15	16
17	18 President's Day	☺	20	21	22	23
24	25	26	27	28	1	2

A 12:23 PM snow scene at the University of Alaska - Fairbanks, Alaska, West Ridge.

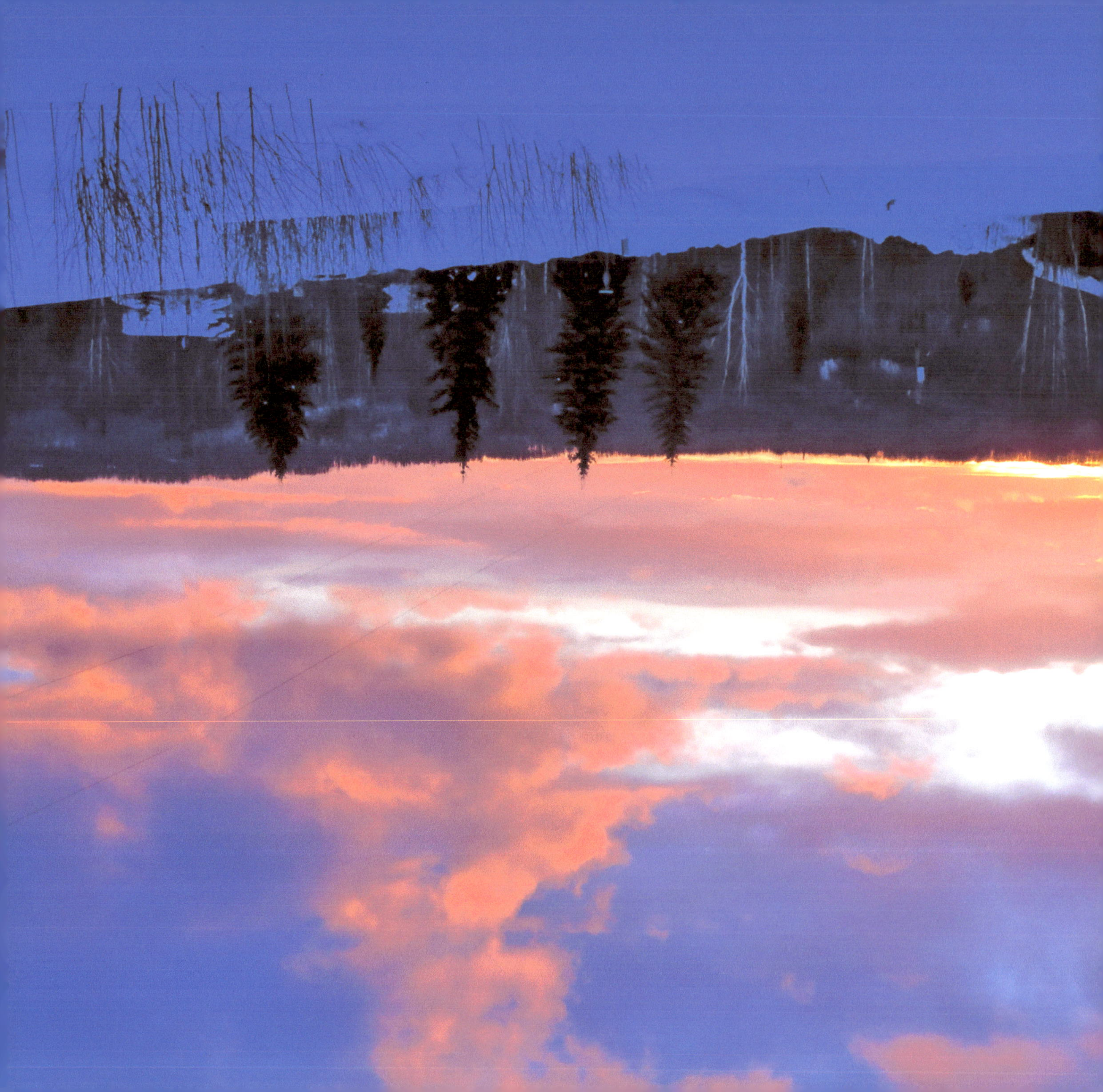

March 2019

Sun	Mon	Tue	Wed	Thu	Fri	Sat
24	25	26	27	28	1	2
3	4	5	6	7	8	9
10 Daylight Saving Time Begin (02:00)	11	12	13	14	15	16
17	18	19	21:58 GMT Vernal Equinox	21	22	23
24	25	26	27	28	29	30
31	1	2	3	4	5	6

A 6:59 PM sunset scene on the Vernal Equinox near Fairbanks, Alaska.

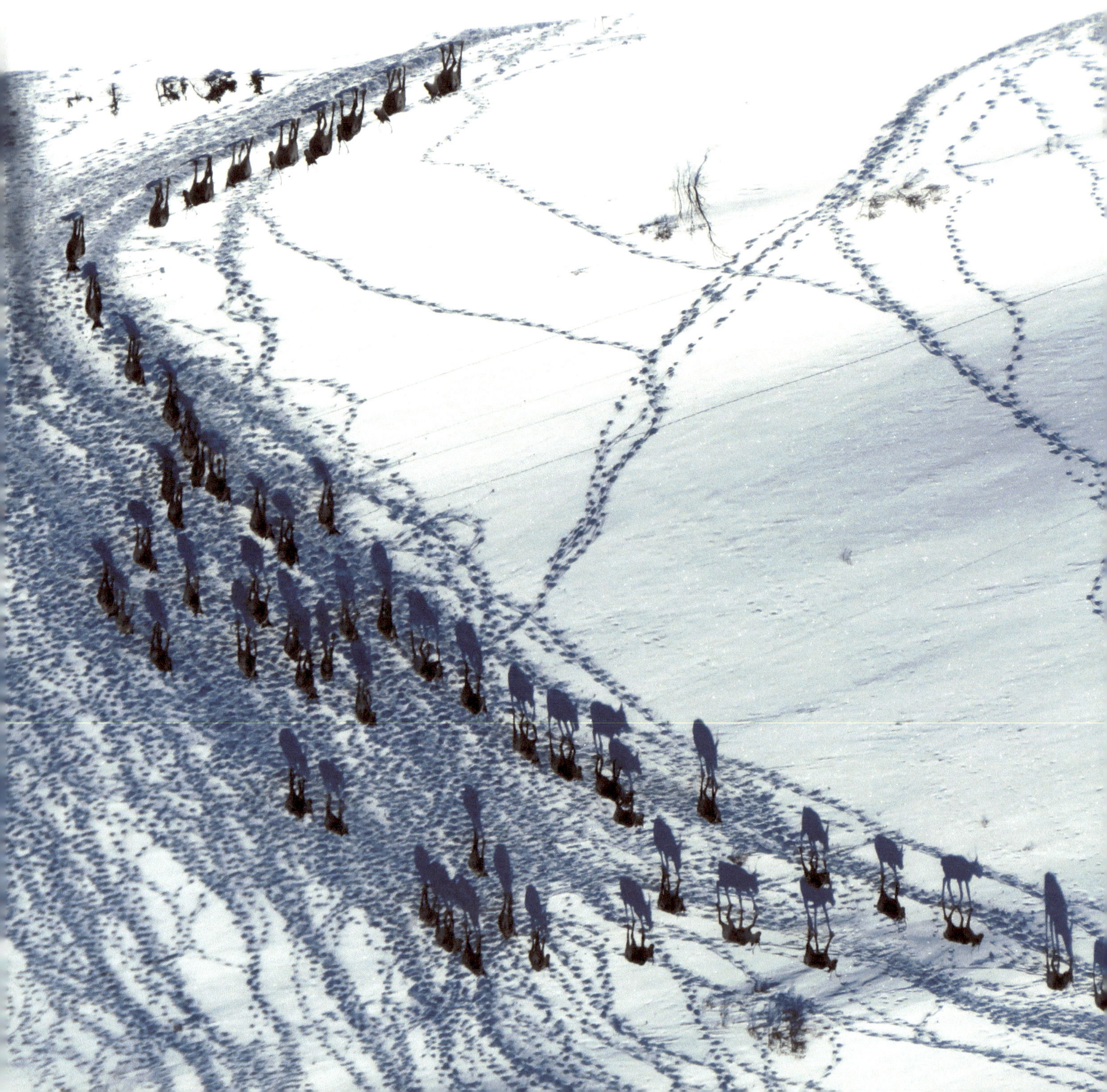

April

2019

Sun	Mon	Tue	Wed	Thu	Fri	Sat
31	1	2	3	4	5	6
7	8	9	10	11	12	13
14	15	16	17	18		20
21 Easter Sunday	22	23	24	25	26	27
28	29	30	1	2	3	4

Caribou (*Rangifer tarandus*) on the move near Eagle Summit, Alaska.

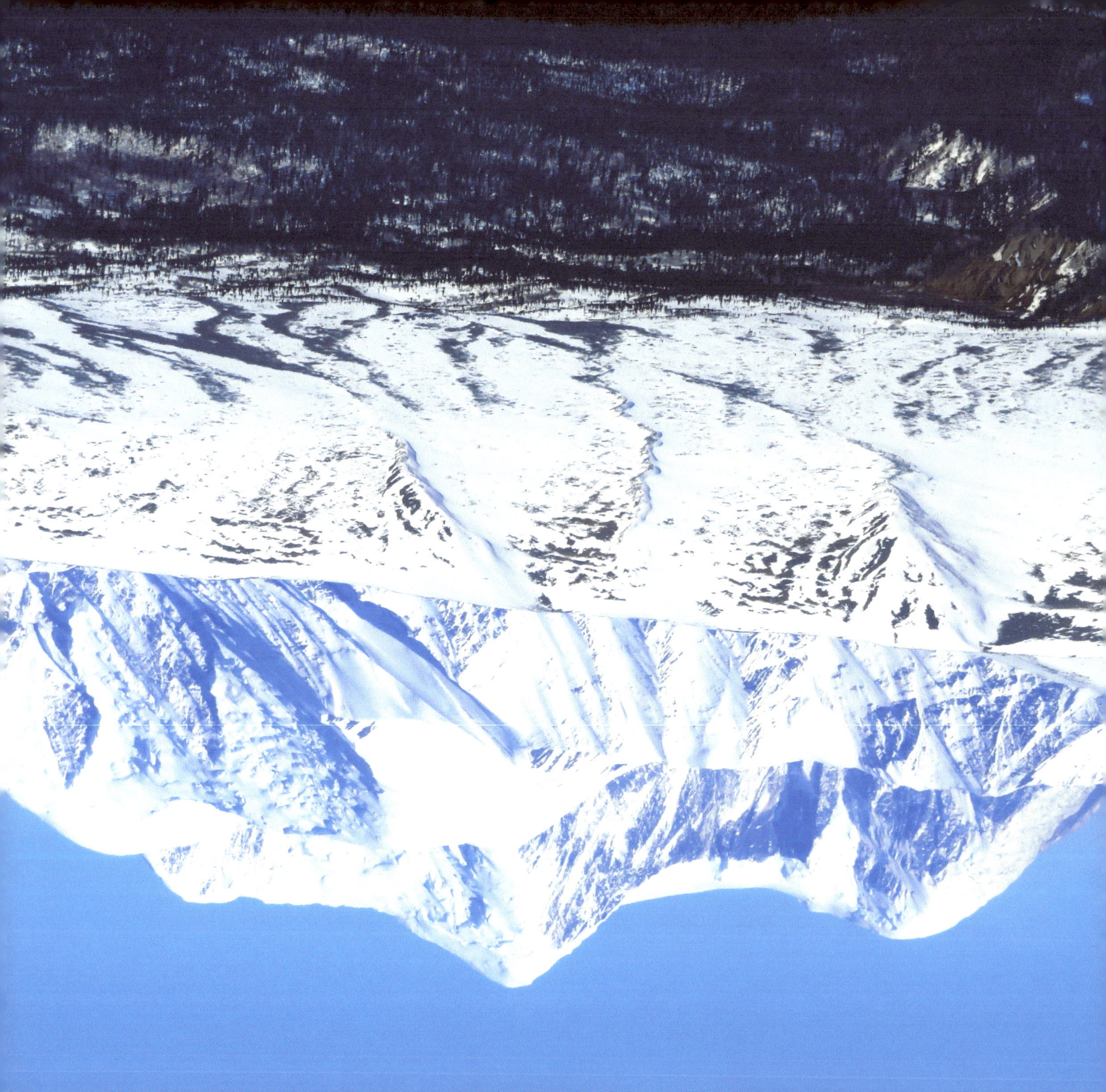

May

2019

Sun	Mon	Tue	Wed	Thu	Fri	Sat
28	29	30	1	2	3	4
5	6	7	8	9	10	11
12 Mother's Day	13	14	15	16	17	
19	20	21	22	23	24	25
26	27 Memorial Day	28	29	30	31	1

An incredible mountain scene in the Alaska Range, from near Summit Lake, Alaska.

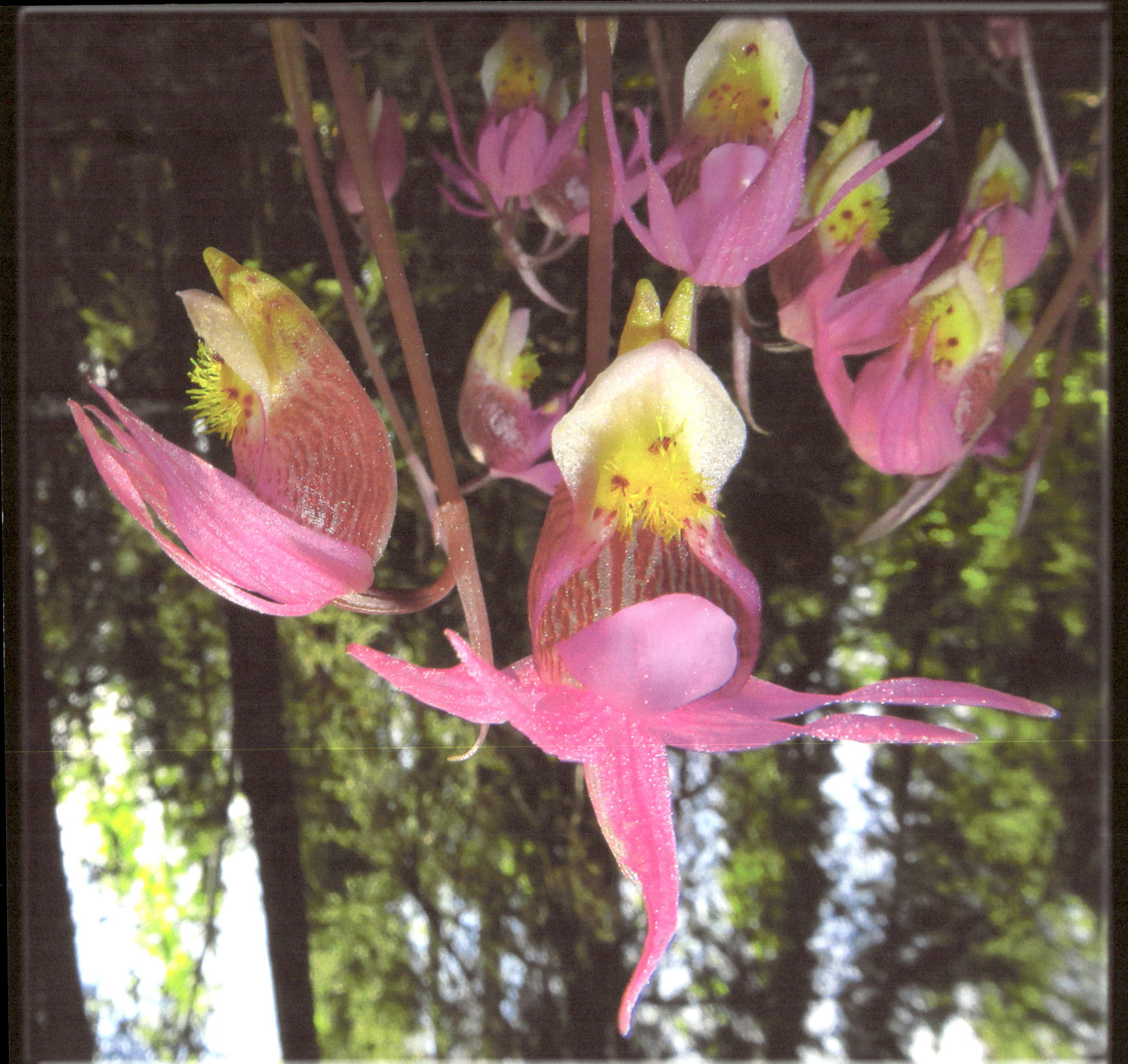

June 2019

Sun	Mon	Tue	Wed	Thu	Fri	Sat
26	27	28	29	30	31	1
2	3	4	5	6	7	8
9	10	11	12	13	14	15
16 Father's Day	☺	18	19	20	21 15:54 GMT Summer Solstice	22
23	24	25	26	27	28	29
30	1	2	3	4	5	6

Calypso Orchids (Calypso bulbosa var. americana) near Fairbanks, Alaska.

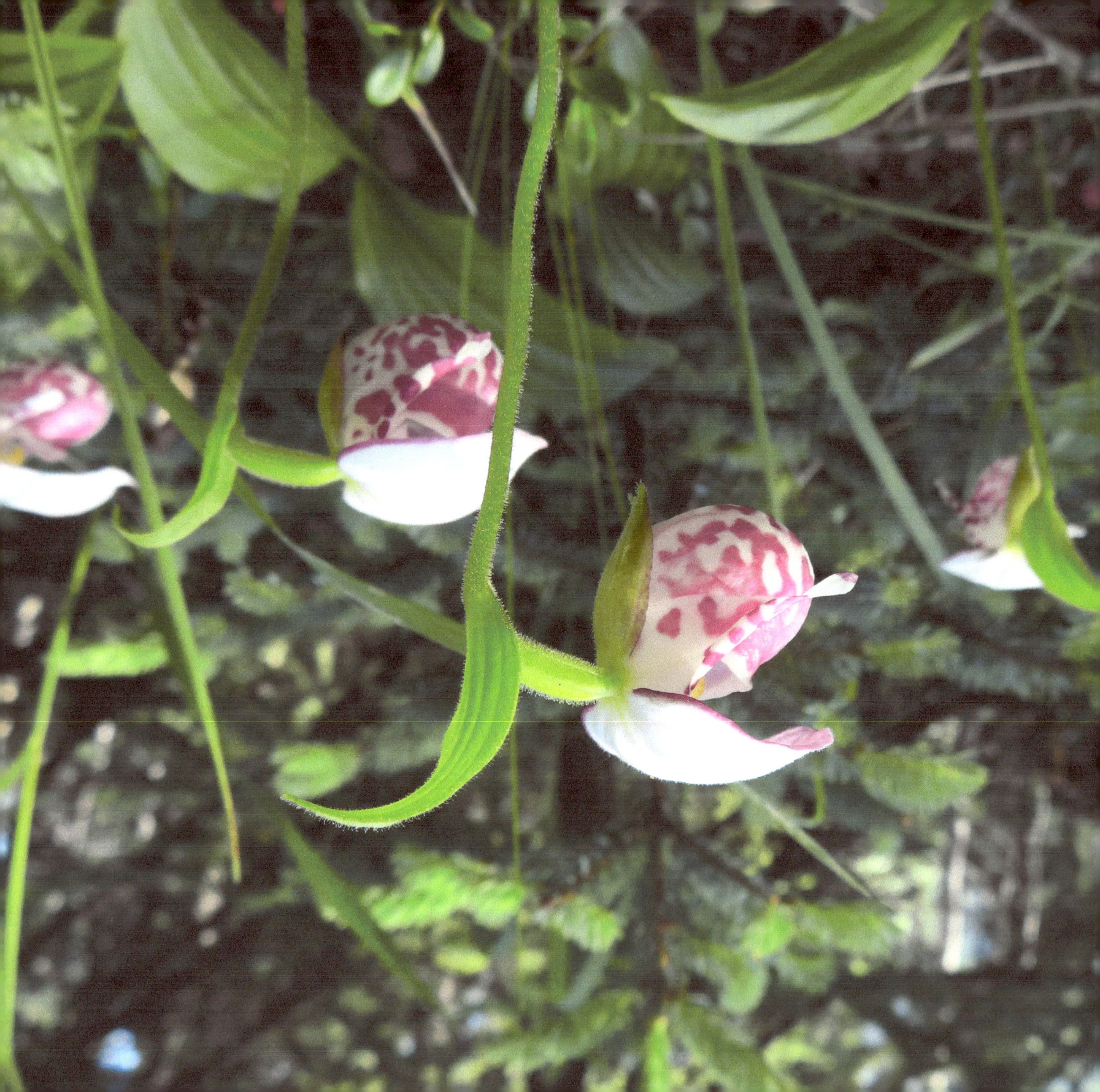

July 2019

Sun	Mon	Tue	Wed	Thu	Fri	Sat
30	1	2	3	4 Independence Day	5	6
7	8	9	10	11	12	13
14	15	🌝	17	18	19	20
21	22	23	24	25	26	27
28	29	30	31	1	2	3

Spotted Lady's Slipper Orchids (*Cypripedium guttatum*) at Grapefruit Rocks near Fairbanks, Alaska.

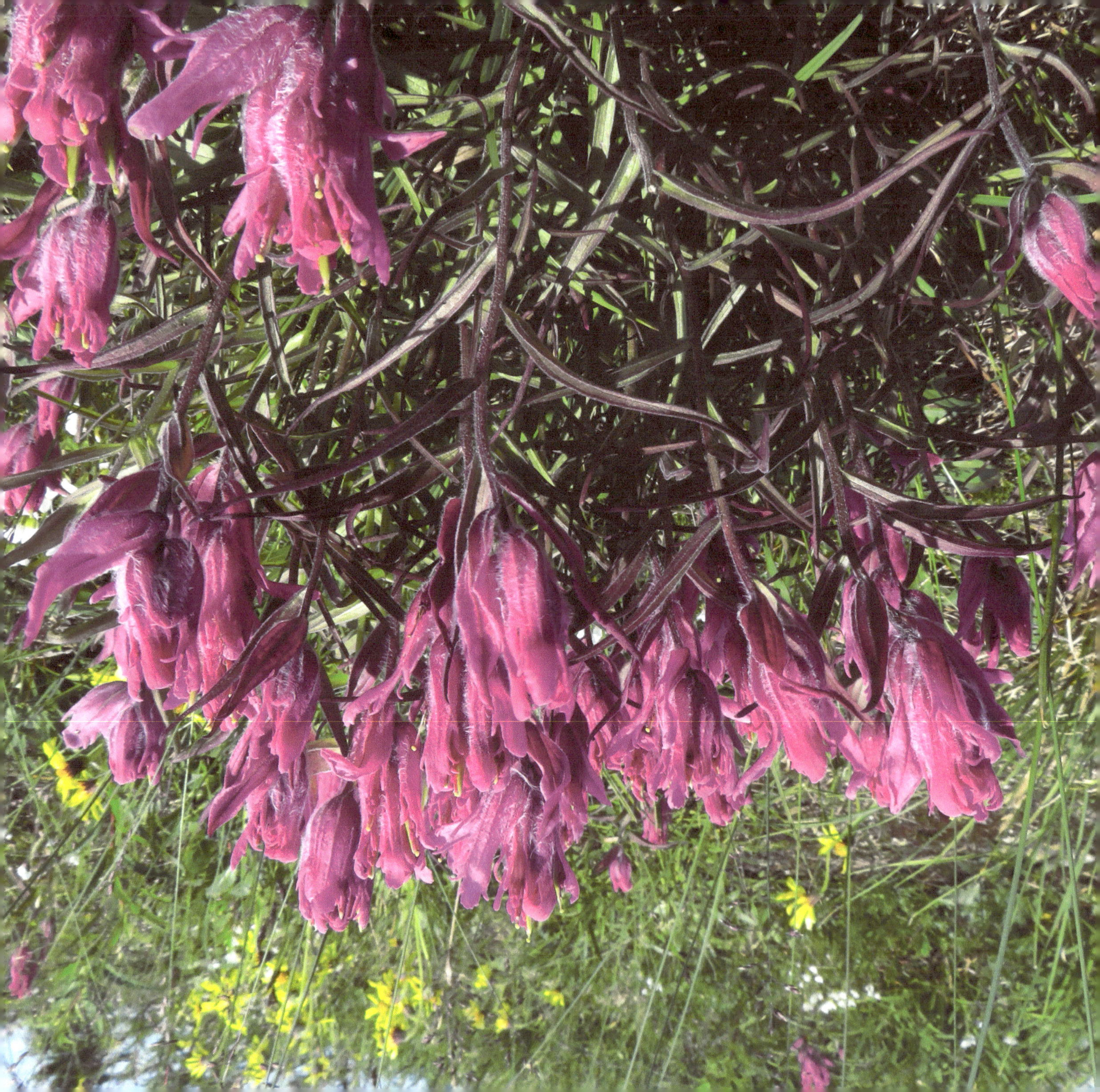

August 2019

Sun	Mon	Tue	Wed	Thu	Fri	Sat
28	29	30	31	1	2	3
4	5	6	7	8	9	10
11	12	13	14	🌝	16	17
18	19	20	21	22	23	24
25	26	27	28	29	30	31

Castilleja elegans (Elegant Indian Paintbrush) at Wickersham Dome near Fairbanks, Alaska.

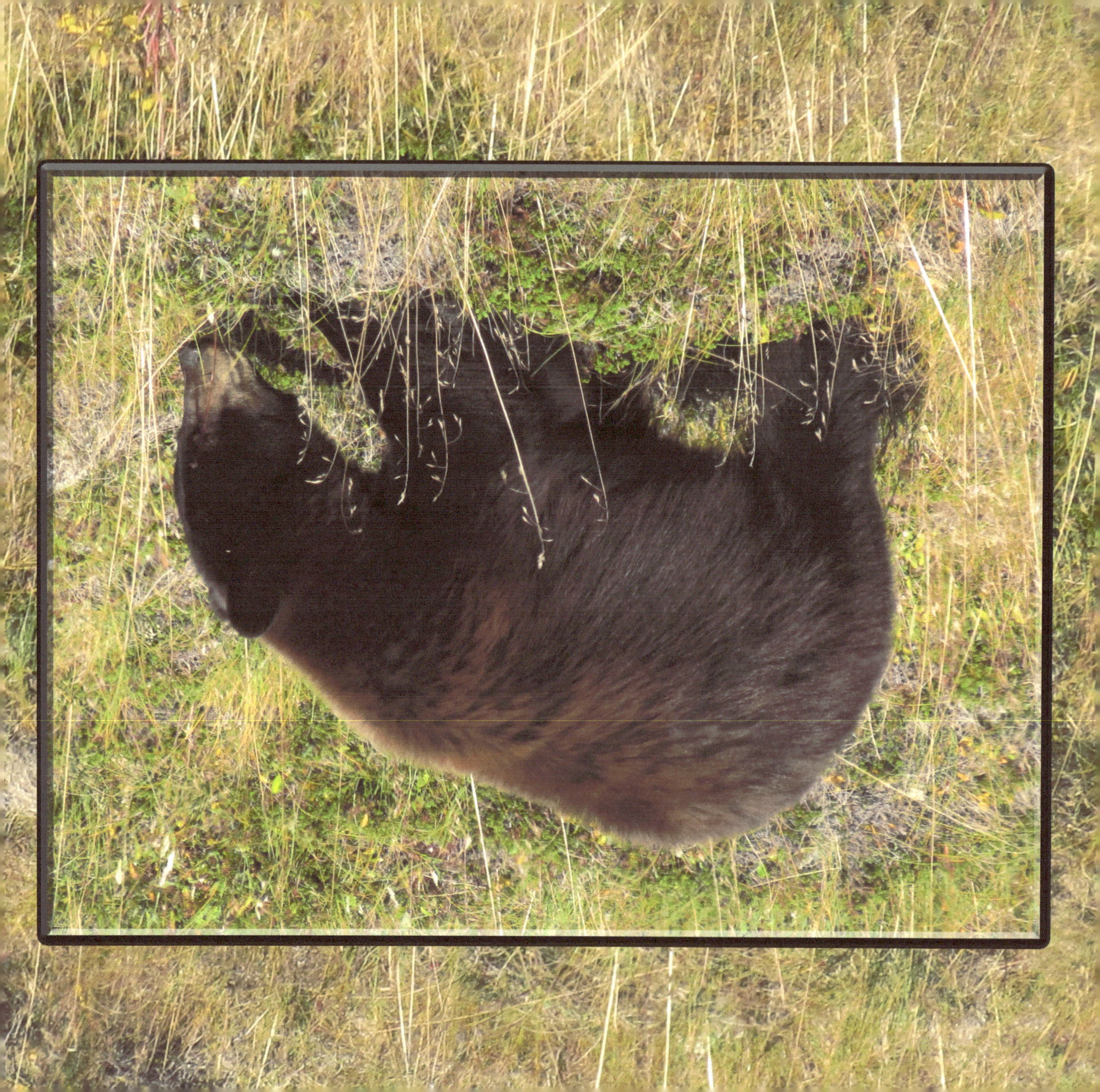

September 2019

Sun	Mon	Tue	Wed	Thu	Fri	Sat
1	2 Labor Day	3	4	5	6	7
8	9	10	11	12	13	
15	16	17	18	19	20	21
22	23 07:50 GMT Autumnal Equinox	24	25	26	27	28
29	30	1	2	3	4	5

Grizzly (Brown) Bear (*Ursus arctos horribilis*) near Eagle Summit, Alaska.

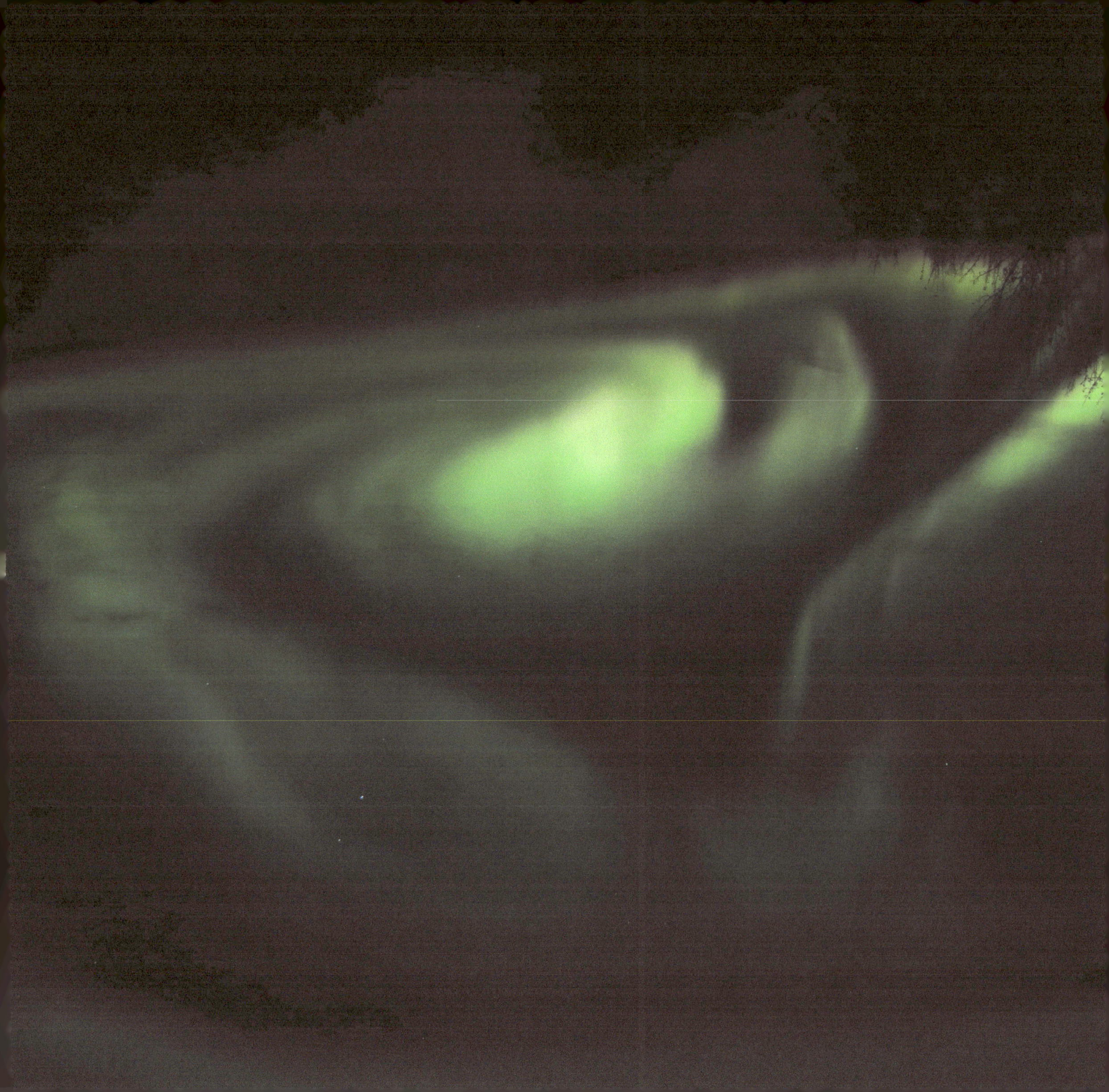

October 2019

Sun	Mon	Tue	Wed	Thu	Fri	Sat
29	30	1	2	3	4	5
6	7	8	9	10	11	12
13	14 Columbus Day	15	16	17	18	19
20	21	22	23	24	25	26
27	28	29	30	31 Halloween	1	2

The Northern Lights (Aurora Borealis) near Fairbanks, Alaska.

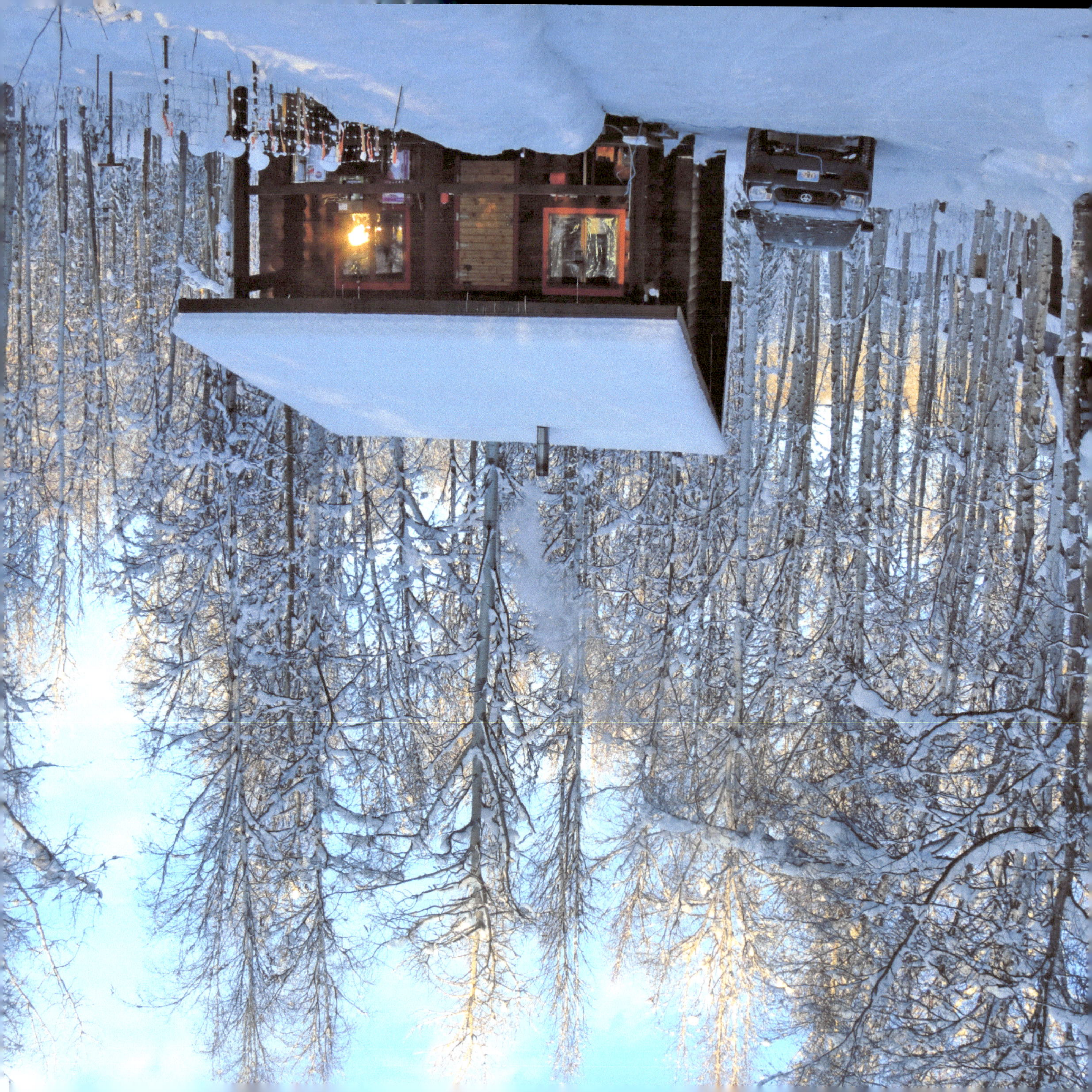

November 2019

Sun	Mon	Tue	Wed	Thu	Fri	Sat
27	28	29	30	31	1	2
3 Daylight Saving Time End (02:00)	4	5	6	7	8	9
10	11 Veteran's Day	🌝	13	14	15	16
17	18	19	20	21	22	23
24	25	26	27	28 Thanksgiving Day	29	30

A cozy log house near Fairbanks, Alaska.

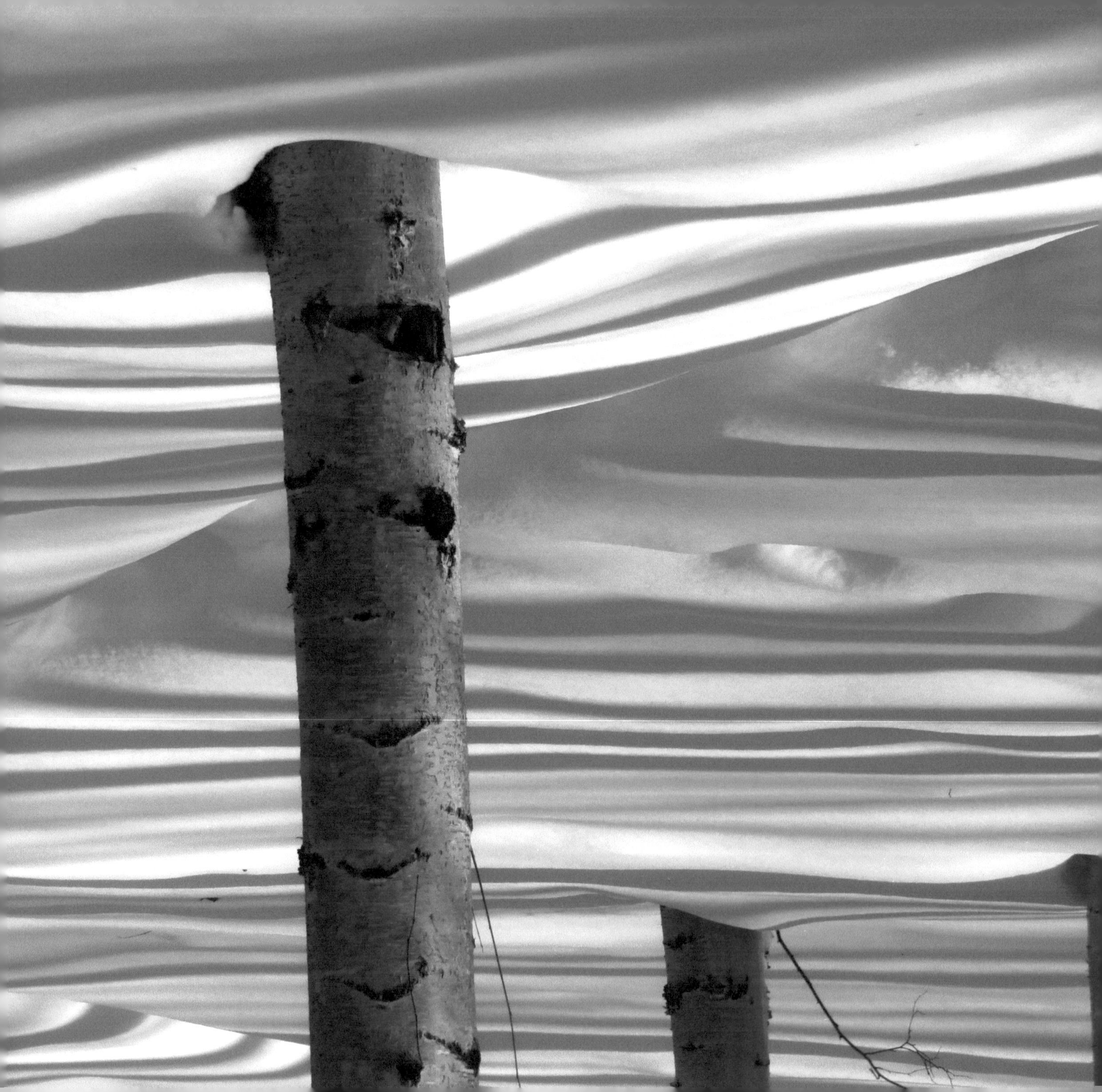

December 2019

Sun	Mon	Tue	Wed	Thu	Fri	Sat
1	2	3	4	5	6	7
8	9	10	11	🌕	13	14
15	16	17	18	19	20	21
22 04:19 GMT Winter Solstice	23	24 Christmas Eve	25 Christmas Day	26	27	28
29	30	31 New Year's Eve	1	2	3	4

Birch tree shadows on the snow near Fairbanks, Alaska.

2019 Phases of the Moon

Universal Time (GMT)

	New Moon				First Quarter				Full Moon				Last Quarter		
	d	h	m		d	h	m		d	h	m		d	h	m
JAN	06	01	28	JAN	14	06	46	JAN	21	05	16	JAN	27	21	10
FEB	04	21	04	FEB	12	22	26	FEB	19	15	54	FEB	26	11	28
MAR	06	16	04	MAR	14	10	27	MAR	21	01	43	MAR	28	04	10
APR	05	08	50	APR	12	19	06	APR	19	11	12	APR	26	22	18
MAY	04	22	45	MAY	12	01	12	MAY	18	21	11	MAY	26	16	34
JUN	03	10	02	JUN	10	05	59	JUN	17	08	31	JUN	25	09	46
JUL	02	19	16	JUL	09	10	55	JUL	16	21	38	JUL	25	01	18
AUG	01	03	12	AUG	07	17	31	AUG	15	12	29	AUG	23	14	56
AUG	30	10	37	SEP	06	03	10	SEP	14	04	33	SEP	22	02	41
SEP	28	18	26	OCT	05	16	47	OCT	13	21	08	OCT	21	12	39
OCT	28	03	38	NOV	04	10	23	NOV	12	13	34	NOV	19	21	11
NOV	26	15	06	DEC	04	06	58	DEC	12	05	12	DEC	19	04	57
DEC	26	05	13	—	—	—	—	—	—	—	—	—	—	—	—

Earth's Seasons – 2019

Universal Time (GMT)

		d	h			d	h	m		d	h	m
Perihelion	Jan	03	05	Equinoxes	Mar	20	21	58	Sept	23	07	50
Aphelion	July	04	22	Solstices	June	21	15	54	Dec	22	04	19

If you enjoyed the photographs shown in this calendar then please be sure to check out our website. It can be found at http://danwiz.com. As long as Daniel is alive he hopes to be able to maintain it.

Kazuya's blog can be found at: http://studiesofplantsandwildlife.blogspot.com or alternately, http://www2.blogger.com/profile/02622643778290337101.

(Revision 1)

www.ingramcontent.com/pod-product-compliance
Ingram Content Group UK Ltd.
Pitfield, Milton Keynes, MK11 3LW, UK
UKHW060115300726
14090UKWH00002B/197
* 9 7 8 0 9 9 6 9 8 1 0 8 8 *